D1239119

# THE BLUE BOOK

### REVISED

Glenn McCracken
New Castle Area Schools
New Castle, Pennsylvania

Charles C. Walcutt
Queens College
Flushing, New York

READING GOALS
Extended Readers for
BASIC READING

J. B. LIPPINCOTT COMPANY
Philadelphia    New York

# CONTENTS

*Illustrations by* Allan Eitzen,
Roland V. Shutts, Carol Wilde.

Copyright ©, 1972, 1966, by J. B. Lippincott Company
Printed in the United States of America
International Rights Reserved
ISBN-0-397-43509-6

10.776.7

## The Pet Frog

Art has a frog on his arm.
The frog hops on his arm.
It hops up to the scarf.

1

Art puts the frog in his scarf.
Sid has part of the scarf.
Art has part of it.

Art puts the frog in the tin can.
The frog can nap in the tin can.
The frog can rest on the scarf.

**Ted**

Ted has a hammer in his hand.
It is his dad's hammer.

His dad has a car.
Ted sat on the car.
Ted hit the fender hard.
The hammer dented the fender.

Ted hid the hammer.
Ted put it in the garden.

Ted sat in his hut.

Ted did not want to dent the fender.

Ted is sad.

Ted's dad is not sad.

His dad is cross.

His dad must get the fender mended.

## Art and His Frog

Art had a red wagon.

Art put his frog in the wagon.

Art ran.

Art ran in the wind.

The wagon went fast.

Art ran faster and faster.

The wagon hit a stump.
The frog hopped off fast.

The frog was not harmed.
It hopped far from the wagon.

The frog hopped to a pond.

It sat in the water.

It did not want to sit in a wagon.

Art was glad the frog was OK.

Art saw his sister, Carmen.
"Carmen, Carmen," said Art.
"Get in the wagon."

Carmen wanted to sit in the wagon.
Carmen got in.
Art and Carmen had fun.

## Lin and Howard Get Lost

It was summer.

Lin and Howard planned a picnic.

14

Howard got a wagon.

Lin got pop and cups.

Howard got nuts and gum.

Lin and Howard left for the forest.
The wind pulled Howard's cap off.
It flipped his cap up on a twig.

Howard got on the wagon.
Lin held it still for him.
The cap was too far up.
Howard did not get his cap.

Howard felt sad.

Howard left his cap on the twig.

Lin and Howard went on.

Lin and Howard had a picnic.
The picnic was on a hill.

The picnic was fun.
Howard forgot his lost cap.

The sun went down.

"Get in the wagon, Lin," said Howard.

Howard pulled the wagon fast.

Lin held on.

Howard pulled her down the hill.

Howard stopped.

The forest was big.

Howard was lost.

Howard did not want to tell Lin.

It was not fun to get lost.

At last Howard saw his cap.
It was still on the twig.
Howard and Lin were not lost now.
"The cap helped us," said Howard.
"The cap led us from the forest."

## Hopper

Hopper was a little rabbit.

Hopper hopped in the tall grass.

The grass was a forest to him.

Hopper had fun in his grass forest.

But Hopper wanted a pal.

Hopper saw a little grasshopper.

"Let's hop," said Hopper.

"Not now," said the grasshopper.

The grasshopper was not his pal.

Hopper went on.

Hopper saw a dog.

It was a big bulldog.

"Let's run," said Hopper.

"Bow wow. Not now," said the dog.

Hopper went on.

Hopper saw a little frog.
"Let's hop," said Hopper.
"Not now, Rabbit," said the frog.
"Ribbit. Ribbit. Ribbit."

And the frog hopped into the water.
Hopper went on.

Hopper saw Brenda.

Hopper sat up and wiggled his paws.

Brenda bent down.

Hopper let Brenda pet him.

Hopper snuggled up to Brenda.
Brenda held Hopper's soft paw.
Hopper sat in Brenda's lap.
Brenda petted him.
At last Hopper had a pal.

## Binker

Binker wanted to rest.

The duck wanted him to get up.

"Get up! Get up!" said the duck.

The duck waddled to the pond.

Binker ran after him.

"It's fun to swim.

Get in the water," said the duck.

"I will sit on the bank," said Binker.

The duck swam on top of the water.
It ducked under the water.
The duck had fun but Binker did not.
"I can swim," said Binker.
"But now I want a drink of milk.
I want to rest, too."

Binker ran back to the basket.
Binker had a drink of milk.

"Ponds are for ducks," Binker said.
"A basket is better for a kitten."
Binker cuddled up and slept.

## A Baseball Game

Dale and Rick came to the game.

Pepper came to the game, too.

It was a baseball game.

Rick had his ball and bat.

Dale had his mitt and the bases.

Dale was at bat.

Dale hit the ball hard.

Dale ran fast to get on base.

Rick ran to tag Dale.

But the man said, "Dale is safe!"

Rick wanted to make a hit, too.
Rick hit the ball.

It went past all the kids.
Rick ran and tagged all the bases.
Rick made a run.

The ball got lost.

It was not on the grass by the lake.

It was not in the ball park.

The kids still had a bat.

But not a ball.

Rick saw Pepper.
Pepper had the ball.
Pepper ran.

The kids ran after him.
Pepper wanted to get in the game.

Pepper ran and sat on base.
"Pepper is safe," said Rick.

"Pepper did not get tagged.
Pepper has made a run."

## Pete's Dog

After dinner, Scott and Sal went to see Pete.

"Will Pete let us see his dog?" asked Sal. "Can we pet him?"

"We can pet him but we can't pick him up," said Scott. "He is too little."

"Pete said his dog is a bulldog,"
said Sal. "Bulldogs are big."

"Bulldogs **get** big," said Scott.
"Pete's dog is just a pup. He is ten
weeks old."

"Here he is," said Scott. "See how little he is."

"We must seem big to him," said Sal.

"He is a little timid," said Pete.
"Pet him. If his neck is rubbed, he
will fall asleep."

Sal rubbed the pup's neck but he
did not fall asleep.

"He needs to be fed," said Pete.
"Let's put warm milk in a pan and
feed him."

It was fun to see Pete's dog lap up the milk. He got his feet in the pan and licked his paws. Now the bulldog will fall asleep.

## Tea and Cake

Kate and Fran made a cake. Fran put a teapot and cups on the table. Kate went to get the cake. Neal and Dean got the seats.

Neal sat down.

"Tea, please," said Neal.

Fran put tea in Neal's cup. Fran
was neat and did not spill a drop.

"Please sit down, Dean," said
Kate. "I will get the cake."

Dean sat down near Neal.

Fran put tea in his cup, too.

"Here's the cake," said Fran.

"Eat the cake, Neal," said Kate.

"Please taste the cake we baked," said Fran.

"We can't eat the cake! It's not a real cake," said Dean.

"It's a mud cake, a pretend cake," said Neal.

"OK," said Kate. "We will get the real cake now. We can all eat it."

The real cake was pink. It tasted sweet. Dean and Neal were pleased. Dean and Neal, Fran and Kate had a feast.

### The Deer

The dream deer
  feed
at the far side of sleep
  but leap
  to the dark
as we wake.

*Adele H. Seronde*

51

## The Airplanes

Gail and Pete went to meet Uncle Matt.

"I want Uncle Matt to see the model plane I made," said Pete. "It is the same as the plane Uncle Matt is on."

"Uncle Matt's plane is a lot bigger than the model plane," said Gail.

"I want to see the big plane land."

"We can see Uncle Matt's plane land from here," said Pete. "But the rain makes it hard to see far."

"I hear it! I can hear it!" said Pete. "And now I can see it too!"

"Uncle Matt's plane seems small. It seems as small as the model plane," said Gail.

Uncle Matt's plane came nearer and nearer. As it came nearer, it seemed to get bigger.

"Wow!" said Pete. "It **is** a big airplane. It has a red tail. I want to paint the model plane. I will paint the tail red."

The big plane landed. Uncle Matt got off the plane. He was glad to see Gail and Pete.

"Do I get a big hug?" asked Uncle Matt.

Pete gave him a hug. Gail sat on his lap.

"Let me see the model airplane,"
said Uncle Matt. "Did Gail make
it?"

"I made it," said Pete. "Now I
want to paint the tail red. I want
it to be the same as the big plane."

"I will be glad to help paint it,"
said Uncle Matt.

"The rain has stopped," said Gail. "Let's wait for the real plane to take off."

"See it get small again," said Pete. "It seems as small as the model plane. Now I cannot see it at all."

## Kites

"Hi!" said Della to her pals.

"Hi!" said Mike. "Let's make kites."

"Fine," said Della. "It will be fun to sail kites in the wind."

"I can't make a kite," said Irene.
"I can," said Mike.

"I can, too," said Della. "And
I will help Irene."

Della got her kite from the closet. It was green with a black kitten on it.

"I like Della's kite," said Irene.

"To make a kite like mine we will need paper, sticks, and paint," said Della.

"We will need rags and twine
for a tail," added Mike.

Mike likes green.

Mike painted a green leaf on
his kite.

Irene painted a bird on her kite.
Della got the twine for the tails.

Della sailed her kite up in the air first.

Mike got on his bike and tried to sail his kite.

"Stop!" called Irene. "The kite will hit the tree."

Mike tried to ride faster. His
kite hit the tree. The line snapped.
Mike felt bad.

Irene and Della helped him get
his kite from the tree.

"The girls can sail the kites,"
said Mike. "I will ride my bike."

## The Lost Hubcap

Mr. Brown's car had a flat tire.
He had to take the hubcap off. He
had to take the old tire off, too.

Mr. Brown put a better tire on his car. It was time to put the hubcap on. But he did not see it.

Mr. Brown hunted and hunted for the hubcap.

"It must be in the sand," said
Mr. Brown.

Mr. Brown dug and dug. But he
did not find the hubcap.

It began to get dark. Mr. Brown got tired. Mr. Brown was hot and tired. He put his hat on the stump and went in to supper.

Mr. Brown forgot his hat. He went back to get it. He got his hat **and** the lost hubcap. The hubcap had rolled under the stump.

"How did I miss it?" asked Mr. Brown.

## The Little Lost Duck

Rose likes to go to the park to read.
Rose goes to a spot near the water
and sits on a blanket. Rose reads
and the ducks swim in the water.

"Come and swim," the ducks call.
But Rose wants to read.

Rose likes to see the little ducks
swim. The little ducks swim in
a line behind the mama duck.

The mama duck and the nine
little ducks swim to the end of the
pond.

Rose sees a little duck. It has
been left behind. His mama calls
but he does not go.

The little duck went up on the
land. He tried to find his mama
and the nine little ducks.

The little duck saw a mole.

"Go back to the water," said
the mole.

The little duck swam in the water.
He swam and swam but he did not
see his mama. He did not find the
nine little ducks.

The little duck swam back to Rose.

"Help me find the ducks," he called.

Rose got up.

"Come here. Come to me," said Rose. "I will help find mama duck and the nine little ducks."

The mama duck missed her little duck.

"I must go back to get my little lost duck," said mama duck.

Rose saw the mama duck.

"Here come the ducks," cried Rose.

The little duck got at the end
of the line.

"I am glad to be back," he said.

### Little Ben

Little Ben went on before
To fill his pail with water.
He went until his feet were sore
But did not find the water.

His sister asked how he did fail
To see the stream beside him,
But he got apples for his pail
And dreamed of sweets inside him.

## Karen and the Little Red Hen

The little red hen lives in part of the barn. Her nest is made of straw. The nest has a brown egg in it.

It is Karen's job to get the eggs. Karen puts her hand under the hen and gets a brown egg. The little red hen does not fuss as Karen gets the egg.

After Karen has the egg, it is time to feed the little red hen. Karen scatters table scraps and grain. The hen jumps off the nest and runs to eat the feed. The red hen bends down and pecks the feed.

Karen feeds her all week. Karen feeds her at seven A.M. and again after supper.

Karen has the brown egg in the green bucket. Karen needs the egg to make lemon cupcakes. Karen will bake the lemon cupcakes for supper.

Karen will save a cupcake for the little red hen.

## Jake

Jake was little and fat. He was
brown and had black stripes. He
had lots of hands and feet.

In the summer Jake lived in the
grass. He ate and slept in a grass
forest. He even made himself a
little grass tunnel to sleep in.

Jake liked to take a nap after
he had eaten. He put up a note near
his tunnel. The note said:

DO NOT
WAKE JAKE

Jake went into his tunnel and
fell asleep.

As Jake slept, it began to rain. It rained hard. The rain got into Jake's tunnel. Jake got wet and cold.

Jake woke up. All his socks were wet and all his feet were cold.

Jake put up a line in the grass. He pinned his socks on the line.

After the rain, Jake's tunnel was
too wet to live in. He needed a
better home. Jake saw a lake of
rain water. He got on a big green
leaf. The leaf floated on the lake
like a boat.

At last Jake came to a spot he
liked. He saw a spot for a new home.
Jake got off the leaf.

It was fall and time to make a winter bed. Jake spun a nest of silk. He covered himself up. He was as snug as a bug in a rug. Jake went fast asleep.

All winter the nest kept Jake safe and warm. He did not feel the cold wind or the frost.

In April Jake woke up. He made a hole in his silk nest. He crawled onto a blade of grass.

But Jake was not the same! Now Jake was a __.

## Fun in the Leaves

Joe and Val liked October.

"See all the leaves," said Val.
"The leaves are all over the garden.
The leaves are gold and red and
brown."

"Let's go and get in the leaves,"
said Joe. "We can rake the leaves
into piles."

October can be cold. Joe got his vest and his red hat. Val put on a warm jacket and her green hat.

Joe even put a coat on the dog. "Rover likes to be kept warm, too," said Joe.

Joe and Val raked the leaves. Val raked hers into a big pile. Joe raked his leaves into five little piles.

Rover was no help. He ran in the leaves. He wanted to find a spot to hide his bone.

Joe had a basket to put the leaves in. Rover saw the basket full of leaves. He put his bone in the basket. Rover got in the basket, too.

Joe and Val did not see him hide in the basket.

It was time to go in.

"Rover, Rover!" called Val.

"Here, Rover!" called Joe.

Rover did not come. He was still.

He did not move.

At last Joe saw Rover's tail.

"Rover fit in the basket but his tail didn't," said Val.

"His tail stuck up like a flag. It told me he was in the basket," said Joe.